Hurting

i.

I'll always write myself these bad reviews

To make sure no-one comes too close again.

ii.

The longer You hold me

The more likely You are to get burnt.

The longer You enjoy me

The more likely I am to cause You harm.

I finally understand

I am Your nicotine.

But

It's me that is hooked on You.

iii.

Darling

I'm just a broken record

With one hell of a scratch.

iv.

There's such a beautiful silence in front of You

And such an elegant crispness.

But all You dream of, is setting fire to Your lungs

To burn the beauty of the silence and disappear into forever.

V.

Sometimes when it's dark

I leave my window open and listen to the world outside.

I hear the cars fly past and wonder about their adventures.

Where are they going?

What are they doing?

Are they in love?

Are they happy?

And it makes me terribly sad.

vi.

I spend so much time wanting to tear myself apart

But

That would be far too visible

And I fear it would make You sad

So, I'll tear us apart instead

And in the end

That is so much more painful

And hits the spot just right.

vii.

Isn't it strange?

The way Autumn is so beautiful

But

As the leaves fall around us

Their colours burning brightly

I can't help but wonder

Why do we find the death of nature so entirely gorgeous?

viii.

'Isn't it strange?'

Thought the moth

'That the most beautiful things in life are the things that kill You.'

He flew one bit closer to that gorgeous flame.

ix.

Sometimes, when your headphones are in

And there is that gap in the music that sits between songs

You can hear people's dreams whispered around You.

Music can often lose its beauty after that.

X.

Dear You

Why do You;

Burn me

Tear me apart

Build me up

Slash at me

Pretend You love me?

When I am always here for You.

All my love.

Always.

Your body.

Xi.

I could explain it to You

How that one less 'x' on Your text makes me panic

How the slight change in Your wording makes me want to hide under the duvet

How that 10-minute delay makes my heart beat too fast

How that time You didn't fully wrap Your hand into mine makes me want to run and run

How my friends not texting me every day means they hate me

How the way my boss looked at me means I'm going to be fired soon

How everyone wants to do things that don't involve me because I'm the worst kind of person

But

I don't

Because these aren't Your problems.

They are mine.

And I know how damned irrational they are

And I know how carefully broken I am

But I'm just a smile to everyone

A secret hurricane of fear.

And I need You ever so much.

xii.

Just because I get drunk on Your kiss every night

Doesn't mean You're my favourite brand.

Xiii.

If too much light can blind You

And too much sound can deafen You

What can too much love do to You?

Xiv.

I can't ever tell if I'm living

Or just being.

Xv.

Keep me hidden

Like a weapon

That You're scared to let loose

But

You always watch

As I swipe right across Your face

And You're holding the gun

But I'm the one with the trigger

And if it goes off.

I don't know who drops first.

Xvi.

I'm sure the moon use to sit a little higher in the sky

I'm sure the rain use to stop on certain days

I swear the sun use to be a little brighter when it finally poked through the clouds.

Xvii.

Where's that world from the movies?

Do people really dance in neon?

Do they live in spontaneity?

Do they flourish in love and flit between adventures?

Or do we all just endure the monotonous normality of life?

Does it get better?

Or is it better, somewhere, out there

And I'm just missing out?

Xviii.

If I set fire to everything we were, are

But clung on ever so tight

Perhaps I'd feel something then.

The burns could be Your forever mark to me.

Xix.

If we have an expiry date

A ticking timer

A countdown clock

Surely, what we do won't change that

Even if I visit my wrists one more time.

I guess there's no place like home.

Xx.

I take one more drag

Maybe I'll quit this soon

But now my lungs are filled

And I can feel them burning

As smoke fills them

I'm full

Full off caffeine and nicotine

And You

I fear when I exhale

I may breathe out the wrong thing.

Xxi.

Sleep, I'm terrified to welcome your warm embrace

For when I allow my eyelids to kiss I see her, every, damn, time

But

It's not a nightmare

It's a gorgeous world

How could it not be?

When her smile fills my vision

Her laugh echoing in the distance.

Perhaps

It is not sleep I am terrified of it seems

Rather the waking to the world alone.

Xxii.

The alcohol

To swirl through my body and numb my mind

To stop me getting in a car at 5am when all I can do is ache for You.

The cigarettes

To burn through my mouth setting fire to my lungs

To stop me thinking about how many days it has been since I tasted Your lips pressed against mine

So why?

Why isn't there anything for my heart

To stop it cracking, crying, shattering.

Xxiii.

I welcome back my old demons

With a wry Cheshire grin and a warm embrace

For these demons I know how to satiate

And I have learnt far too well how to hide them from the world.

Xxiv.

The silence of the buzzing room

Only broken by the click of a lighter

The burning of that sweet distraction

Everyone's staring.

But You haven't noticed that You're crying yet.

Xxv.

My shadow looks so sad strewn across the ceiling

For it no longer has Yours to dance with through the night.

Xxvi.

I often wonder if they made a mistake when they were dealing out lives

Perhaps they slipped and put the one meant for me in someone else's world

For I dream of fields and music

Dancing and summer

With those small American diners and a head resting upon my shoulder

I dream of being hand in hand with You and milkshakes resting in front of us

Mostly, however,

I dream of being the first choice

The main pick

Being good enough

For in this life, I am not.

And I think someone has all my love.

xxvii.

I wish this fire,

The one in my lungs,

The one I press so regularly to my skin,

Would burn everything out of me down to my core

Until there was nothing left.

37 feels like a long way off.

Longing

i.

Light me up darling

Make me that $2 bad mistake

And let me burn through Your lungs

Your soul

Like that cheap cigarette.

Only I'm more consumed by Your lips

Than that smoke filled regret

Or that boy You use to see

Lock up my lips.

But give her a spare key.

ii.

Treat me like a preacher

Confess to me Your sins

Tell me 'x' marks the spot

Then stain me with Your lips.

Darling I built our house on kerosene

And now I'm burning this down.

iii.

I used to wonder about the allure of hunting hurricanes

But

As I once again detach myself from my body

Sitting back to look at the destruction You leave

As You tear through what use to be my heart and soul,

I realise what a beautiful sight it is.

To watch something of such pure nature and power

Completely overwhelm everything I thought was me

The worst (best) part of it all

Is how much beauty Your hurricane adds to my world.

iv.

How am I meant to find my way back to You

When the stars are all blocked out by neon?

<u>V.</u>

Oh

How I wish You were as sure as the shore

As present as the rocks

But, God

I just wish we could be as eternal as the moon

And spend our life making everything crash.

vi.

Kiss me like the sunset sets its lips upon the horizon

Set fire to my lips and burn away at my thoughts

For,

When You press Your mouth against mine

There is nothing left of me

And everything becomes us.

vii.

Inhale me

Completely.

I want You to consume me.

In the most poisonous of ways.

viii.

Reignite my scars with Your lips,

My heart

My wrists

They're all Yours.

ix.

Words dance across my tongue

Ready to shoot like stars across the sky

Resembling burning fire, they scold my skin

And

Then

Just like the dying lights in the skies

They flicker out before Your eyes.

X.

Darling,

When You held my hand

You showed me that home could be a person too.

xi.

I traced a map on Your skin with my fingers once

Now I need You back to help me find my way back home.

xii.

The first time I saw You my mind screamed run

It just made the mistake of not telling my heart which way.

xiii.

I want to live somewhere that has a book store and a wine bar in one

So, my body and soul can become intoxicated together.

Xiv.

Psychology for the confused

Philosophy for the loveless

Poetry for the lovers.

XV.

I dream of having that kind of life

The kind You see in those beautiful American shows

Where the leaves fall around in a Golden hue

And their days are worthy to be narrated in beauty

By distant voices surveying what a gorgeous chance at life they have.

Xvi.

I crave liquor filled nights

Coated with haze and mistakes

All beautifully burned into my flesh like ink.

Xvii.

I miss You when I'm alone

I burn with jealousy for the lipstick that gets to press against Your lips

I fill with envy for the covers that get to keep You warm at night.

Just whisper to me that You love me

Because my name feels so safe on Your tongue.

Xviii.

What an untapped resource love could be

If it wasn't for its very finite amount.

Xix.

I had a dream that we held hands in the rain

But there was an umbrella and I hated it

Because I had to share You with it

And I woke up crying.

And I remembered that time I bought You roses

That tinted my glasses some more.

I don't know if I miss You, miss missing You, or miss that I never missed You at all.

Xx.

I long for lips to cling to me

Like that lost drop of Your favourite drink

To stain me with Your taste

So I become intoxicated all day.

Xxi.

It wasn't her words that showed me love

It was the way she pressed music against my lips at 5am

How she opened my wings and encouraged me to fly

In loving You I learnt how to not hate myself

For all I long for is to drift away with You

And wake up not knowing where I end and You begin.

Xxii.

As my fingers lock with Yours

I remember that each moment with You is a snowflake

Perfectly unique

Destined to melt away

I cannot wait for the eternal blizzard to come.

Xxiii.

I smelt someone else wearing Your perfume today

It stopped me dead in my tracks

I felt an anger swell within me

No-one else should have it

I only want it to belong to You and for it to be Yours alone.

Just like I am.

Xxiv.

I want to photograph every smile of your world.

Xxv.

As the leaves begin to fall into Autumn

I feel that familiar seasonal mood sweep down over me

The one that smells like pumpkin and looks like a 3 dollar razor.

And there You are with your eyelashes that flicker like seasons,

But, You don't smell like pumpkin,

Rather, something new.

And oh so addictive

It fills with me want,

With lust and fire.

The mood I once knew is swept aside

Like leaves from a path

As you burn through my senses

My emotions.

And I pray.

Oh God

Oh Darling.

That I don't have to quit you.

My new nicotine.

My personal brand of heroin.

With fire in her hair

And my eyes in her soul.

Loving

i.

He wanted to be her knight, not just for a night

But for always.

ii.

Where the grey skies hang

And Your pretty in pink lips pressed against mine

That's where You'll find me.

iii.

My strewn canvas is wiped clear

And painted afresh with serenity

As my lips draw ever closer to Yours.

How beautifully these miles fade away.

iv.

"I am no longer afraid of the dark." The Young man whispered,

"For with the dark comes the stars, and I have come to see that they are the world reflecting her eyes, for those not lucky enough to have seen them up close."

V.

All of the sun's rays pressing down upon me will never warm my skin like the flicker of Your lips and fingers against my body.

vi.

Hold my hand and come and find home with me.

vii.

I took You to the place where my heart sings, never expecting You to add Your own melody but, the harmony You made of it was so beautiful.

viii.

I sometimes look at other couples and wonder if they see their other half the way I see You.

I hope so.

Everyone deserves to feel and be looked at, like, to someone, they are the most beautiful being in the world.

ix.

In a world so flat and stagnant

That had been left out on the side for so long

You added bubbles to it and made the universe fizz.

X.

I don't want her to search for my love in things that the ordinary can do. For my love for her isn't the bland You can find with enough money but, rather, with the hours spent searching for the right flower amongst the field of beauty. The gifts given whilst I hold my breath and await her laughter. The look on my face when I give to her my latest find. It is never money I put into these things. It is all of my love for her. This is all I need her to search for.

xi.

His legs ran as fast as they could, with a million laughs caught in his throat, as she disappeared into the fire reds of Autumn on the edge of the world. There she stopped. She raised up His hood, on Her hoody and waited. Then, the boy finally arrived, and neither the seas nor the colours of the world held any power for him because, she had waited, for him, to hear of his laughter and love for her.

xii.

I would paint You every day with my words to keep every syllable of You immortal.

xiii.

The world has never been as silent to me as when Your laughter fills the air.

I'd spend a lifetime spilling drinks on myself to never hear another sound.

xiv.

I wish my words could fill Your mind and flow as smoothly as the silk hot chocolate You sit across from me with.

XV.

It is no longer the end I see in my future

Rather

The rest of forever holding Your hand.

xvi.

It is in the evenings where poetry fills my ears and the sun torments the horizon, that I wish we could make love filled clouds of air from our lips to touch the blossoming night sky.

xvii.

Hold my words within Your lips as we breathe warm clouds up to the ice sky.

xviii.

It is with each step towards the setting sun, where the wind plays gently with Your hair, that I once again lose all consciousness of myself.

xix.

Give me the smell of the sea, Your laughter floating across the air, the warmth of You near me and, I will be richer than any man may dare dream.

XX.

True love is the most decadent hot chocolate on the darkest nights and the most exquisite cocaine in the beautifully neon filled ones.

xxi.

In our pasts two people have kicked leaves, brushed away tears from a cheek, had the tingling of that first hand hold, with two other love lost souls. All so we can share each and every one of those experiences today, together.

xxii.

With every fresh frosty breath reaching up to the clouds I lose myself.

With every scenic dream we stumble upon I lose myself.

With every moment we spend here I lose myself.

But.

With every moment of loss.

I become even more us.

Just when I thought we couldn't fall in love any further.

xxiii.

From every clouded castle top, to each frosted dessert.

For every laugh spent and warm drink devoured.

From every second of walking leading to every hour of fun.

For every kiss shared and every memory burnt into my soul.

It is You I will remember the most.

And how each giggle, each missed shot, each dizzy spin, lit my world up brighter than any Sun could dream of.

xxiv.

It is not the castle tops glistening in the clouds that fill my thoughts.

Nor is it the miles of beauty.

Not the markets glistening with festive wonder.

Neither is it the trees adorned with light.

It is You and, the way Your eyes lit up when we laughed,

The memories we set into our souls like tattoos painting pictures of music, fear, exploring and discovering a whole new world.

It is Your name set across my soul I leave with.

XXV.

I will stumble over a hundred thousand words,

Drain a hundred vocabularies,

Consume a thousand dictionaries,

And I still won't be able to find the words to tell You what it feels like when You smile in Your sleep.

xxvi.

Show me more beauty, than a hot drink, Your embrace and, an afternoon with nothing floating ahead of us.

xxvii.

It is the inner wolf crying at the full moon that I see in You.

The world horse chasing the thunder across the plains.

The lioness roaring at the wild.

All of these things are the world that I love in You

xxviii.

She had eyes you would tear your whole world apart for.

xxix.

If raindrops were my dreams falling from the stars

Then You are the Earth, my love,

Catching each and every one, holding them

Keeping them safe.

XXX.

It is not a city that lasts forever.

Nor is it a mere kingdom.

Rainstorms will be blown away to nothing.

And forests will be sunk into the seas.

But.

The way You smile when I trip

The way I miss You when You're gone.

These, will last for an eternity.

xxxi.

Every moment that the sun sits upon Your eyelashes is an eternal golden hour.

xxxii.

There, in a castle

With the moon lighting our forever,

I promised You my love

And there it will stay

With us

With the moon and that star freckled broken fortress.

Forever immortal.

Forever ours.

Forever You and I.

xxxiii.

When I wake before Her

The sun breaking through

I dream of a million situations;

To stay in this moment,

To lay a kiss upon Her lips

To wake Her and run into the world chasing the sun.

A million dreams.

All for Her.

xxxiv.

Tell me

Of the world we will make

The stars we will see

The waves we will run to

The storms we will run from.

Tell me of us. Tell me of Your dreams of our future.

XXXV.

There are fleeting moments

When I sit wrapped in blankets

And the plants steal Your focus

That I love You even more than I ever thought was possible.

xxxvi.

It is not an ask of ours, for the sun to rise, for the moon to glow, for the waves to crash or the land to grow. These are the promises for us.

From the universe.

As is my love for You.

xxxvii.

Every day I remember a little bit more of how those fairy tales talk of love.

xxxviii.

I would cover notebooks in scrawl, coffee stains and the distant linger of nicotine

To try and put into words, sights, senses, the way Your lips feel after they have been parted from me for too long.

xxxix.

Look for me in the rain amongst the trees

The ripples in the still

Lose me in dance music and fast heart beats

And find me at home in Your soul.

XXXX.

If I arrived at the gates knowing nothing other than the depths of her eyes, I would stand there a happy man.

Xxxxi.

Darling

Let's take to the skies

And see how many languages we can spell our love in.

Xxxxii.

Have You ever tried to write a love poem?

To play with all the clichés and still not get close to explain

How Her eyes danced in the moonlight

How Her lips flickered so faintly across yours so faintly that first moment they touched

How Her fingers traced their way across your skin marking You forever

How She set fire to everything you imagined

And burnt through your every thought

Filling every second of the day

Oh, how Her laughter made your soul swell

And you'd do anything to make her smile

Because

She was everything that was beautiful in the world

And the world was ever so much more illuminated by Her mere presence.

I have

I have tried countless times.

And the words don't even come close.

Xxxxiii.

The words floated through the fragile air above their bed like smoke

Whispers between lovers at 12:00am laced with nicotine, lust and whiskey.

"I love you."

Xxxxiv.

Give me the waves

Your lips

North Devon

And tequila

And I will have more than any conqueror ever dared dream of.

Xxxxv.

With each glisten of rain set against the light of the lamppost,

I see your smile when the songs you love play on the radio.

Printed in Poland
by Amazon Fulfillment
Poland Sp. z o.o., Wrocław